T5-AQT-727

30

SPECTACULAR
SALADS

anything but ordinary

**Shop Smart.
Cook Smart.**

BY KELLY DONLEA
~ with Carolyn Coblentz ~

KELLYOONLEA

Acknowledgments

WITH SPECIAL THANKS
TO MY SISTER, THE OCCASIONAL
VEGETARIAN AND FOREVER
VEGETABLE PRO, FOR HER
PARTICIPATION IN THIS BOOK.

ADDITIONAL THANKS TO MY MOTHER,
WHO BROUGHT VEGETABLES FROM HER GARDEN
TO OUR TABLE EVERY NIGHT AND
TAUGHT US TO LOVE THEM.

TO KRISTIN ENSTROM OF ENSTROM & WHEAT
PHOTOGRAPHY AND WENDY ENGELKING OF
STUDIO ONE ELEVEN DESIGN, MY PRODUCTION TEAM
WHO SERVED NOT JUST AS CREATIVE CONSULTANTS,
BUT AS TASTE-TESTERS, SOUNDING BOARDS
AND EDITORS IN THE PROCESS OF
BRINGING 30 SPECTACULAR
SALADS TO LIFE.

Recipe Index

Recipe Index

Introduction

30 SPECTACULAR SALADS
anything but ordinary

Salads can mean different things to different people.

For some, salads and soup are the only meals that need to exist. For others, salads are an "extra" course that make their way into a meal almost unnoticed. "Salads" is a very encompassing category, one that can become so much more interesting, curious, and exciting when we consider the wide variety of vegetables that are available for us to mix and match.

The colorful produce offered on this Earth deserves so much more than to be doused in fat. We think it should be showcased and partnered with other fresh ingredients to bring out the best flavors and benefits. With the recipes in this book, you get your broccoli, your spinach, your asparagus... in ways that are so inventive you may forget you're "eating your vegetables."

To those who love salads as a main course, many a meal can be found in this book. We include an equal amount of winners for the most-loved side dish brought to a barbecue or potluck. This book also provides new opportunities for using the results of your vegetable and herb gardens, as well as a fresh take on your traditional Mexican, Italian, and Thai fare.

Each recipe in this book takes a wide variety of down-to-earth ingredients and pairs flavors that are in some cases so simple, in some cases so extraordinary, and in all cases fantastic and full of flavor — often without requiring much in the way of dressing. And so, with our apologies to their makers, we invite you to throw away your mayonnaise and salad dressings. With *30 Spectacular Salads: Anything but Ordinary*, you'll learn to make delicious, delightful salads and dressings that showcase beautiful fresh produce and bring fabulous flavor to your table, every night of the week.

Light &
Delicious

Beet, Goat Cheese, and Red Onion Salad

For this colorful, healthful, and tasty salad, pickle fresh beets in a brine of 1/4 cup cider vinegar, a few cloves, and a tablespoon each of oil, salt, and sugar. Or, simply buy canned pickled beets.

Makes 4-6 servings

INGREDIENTS

1 cup coarsely chopped walnuts
2 tablespoons butter
1 tablespoon sugar
7 ounces pickled beets, diced
4 ounces goat cheese, crumbled
1 cup celery, chopped
2 tablespoons cider vinegar

In a pan on stove, melt butter and cook walnuts with sugar until fully cooked and coated, stirring often. Cool walnuts. Combine walnuts with remaining ingredients in bowl and chill before serving.

Edamame Salad

There's a lot to like about edamame (immature soy beans). They're consistent in firmness, pretty, tasty, and packed with nutrients. One 3-ounce serving contains 12 grams of protein — the same amount you'd get from one egg — as well as a substantial amount of fiber, omega fatty acids, folic acid, and vitamin K. Enjoy this salad for the fun you'll have eating it as well as the knowledge that you're doing yourself a healthy deed.

Makes 4 servings

INGREDIENTS

12 ounces edamame, shelled
1 teaspoon garlic salt
1 cup mandarin oranges, mostly drained
3 ounces water chestnuts, diced
¼ cup sliced almonds
1 tablespoon soy sauce
Juice of 1 lime

Season edamame with garlic salt. Blend with remaining ingredients and chill.

3

Tomato Avocado Salad

This salad is a wonderful example of letting the true flavors of food work together to make a great meal. With very few ingredients, you get a flavorful combination of rich and light and a beautiful color contrast you can enjoy on so many levels. This salad serves well with crusty bread, as an accompaniment to flank steak or other meat, or as a meal all its own.

Makes 6–8 servings

INGREDIENTS

6 ounces goat cheese, thinly sliced
2 tomatoes, halved and sliced
2 avocados, sliced
1 teaspoon salt
1 teaspoon black pepper
1 tablespoon balsamic vinegar
1 tablespoon olive oil

Slice tomatoes and avocado into wedges. Slice goat cheese into rounds. Arrange alternating slices on a serving dish; season with salt and pepper. Drizzle with oil and vinegar.

Crunchy Green Bean Salad

This salad packs a crunch! Here we feature green beans the way they are meant to be enjoyed — not smothered in oil, but paired with light, sweet, crunchy accompaniments. This beautiful, healthful, colorful salad is a great addition to any meal.

Makes 6 servings

INGREDIENTS

1 pound green beans
2 celery stalks, diced
2 tablespoons onion, diced
½ red bell pepper, chopped
1 green bell pepper, chopped
⅓ cup white vinegar
1 teaspoon garlic salt
1 tablespoon sugar
1 tablespoon fresh parsley, minced
Slivered almonds, if desired

Blanch green beans for 2 minutes in boiling water to soften slightly. Slice into 1-inch pieces. Combine with remaining ingredients and chill. Top with slivered almonds if desired.

5

Creamy Cucumber Salad

Fresh and crunchy...with an attitude. This great combination of flavors and seasonings work together to present one of summer's freshest fare in an elegant experience. Serve with pita bread or as an accompaniment to most any main course.

Makes 4 servings

INGREDIENTS

1 tablespoon olive oil
1 teaspoon hot sauce
2 teaspoons lemon juice or white vinegar
8 ounces Greek yogurt
2 cloves garlic, finely chopped
2 cups cucumber, peeled, seeded, and sliced
½ teaspoon dill
1 teaspoon sugar

Combine oil, sugar, lemon juice, and hot sauce in a bowl. Fold in yogurt slowly and mix completely with the oil. Add the garlic and the cucumber. Garnish with dill and chill.

Toe - May - Toe? Toe - Mah - Toe?
The question of whether the tomato is a fruit
or a vegetable has actually been debated in the
United States Supreme Court. In 1893, in Nix v. Hedden,
it was ruled that a tomato will be identified as,
and thus taxed as, a vegetable. The court did
acknowledge, however, that, botanically
speaking, a tomato is a fruit.

~ Wikipedia

Tomato, Kalamata, and Bleu Cheese Salad

This is one of those simple combinations of ingredients that packs a huge punch in the flavor department. This salad serves well with a side of crusty bread, pita bread, or even tortilla or pita chips.

Makes 4 servings

INGREDIENTS

2 tomatoes, diced
½ red onion, diced
1 tablespoon balsamic vinegar
1 tablespoon olive oil
4 ounces crumbled bleu cheese
8 ounces kalamata olives, pitted and chopped

Combine all ingredients. Serve chilled.

Carrot and Napa Cabbage Salad

Often used as a salad accompaniment, we are pleased to present cabbage and carrots as the shining stars of this delicious, zesty salad. Arugula can be substituted for the cabbage for similar, tasty results.

Makes 4 servings

INGREDIENTS

4 medium carrots, sliced into rounds
2 cups Napa cabbage, chopped
¼ cup feta cheese, crumbled

Combine carrots, arugula, and feta. Top with Basil Dressing (below).

Basil Dressing
INGREDIENTS

1 tablespoon olive oil
2 tablespoons vinegar
3 fresh basil leaves, finely chopped
⅛ teaspoon pepper
¼ teaspoon salt
2 teaspoons lemon juice
1 large clove garlic, pressed

Combine or blend all ingredients and chill.

KELLYDONLEA

Black Bean Asparagus Salad

This multi-purpose salad works as a salsa, with chips, on its own as a meal, or as a garnish for grilled chicken or meat. The beautiful color combination is a treat for any table.

Makes 4-6 servings

INGREDIENTS

½ pound (approximately 7 spears) asparagus
¾ cup cooked black beans, drained and rinsed
2 tablespoons white wine vinegar
2 tablespoons red onion, finely diced
1½ teaspoons jalapeno, finely diced
1 clove garlic, minced
1 tablespoon fresh Italian parsley, minced
1 tomato, seeded and diced
¼ teaspoon ground cumin
½ teaspoon salt

Blanch asparagus for 2 minutes in boiling water. Immediately drain and rise with cold water. Dice asparagus into ¼-inch rounds. Combine with remaining ingredients. Chill before serving.

9

Chick Pea Salad with Mangoes and Rosemary

Long popular in India and Mediterranean locales, garbanzo beans (chick peas) have become increasingly popular worldwide as a food high in protein, fiber, and vitamins, while still low in fat. They make a great salty base for a salad that pairs well with many sweet counterparts. We've combined them here with mangoes, parsley, and rosemary for a delicious, healthy, sweet-and-savory flavor combination.

Makes 4 servings

INGREDIENTS

1 teaspoon parsley
1 teaspoon salt
1 clove garlic, minced
1 teaspoon olive oil
1 pound cooked or canned garbanzo beans, drained and rinsed
3 tablespoons minced fresh rosemary
1 mango, peeled and cut into small cubes
½ cucumber, seeded, peeled, and cubed
1 tablespoon sweet vinegar such as cider, or fruit infused

Combine all ingredients and chill.

Traditional...
Anything
But Ordinary

Strawberry Black Olive Caesar Salad

Here we combine a basic Caesar with black olives and strawberries to give this traditional salad some added Vitamin C — all shown off with a great color combination to boot.

Makes two large entrée salads, or a side serving for 4-6.

INGREDIENTS

4 one-inch thick slices day-old Italian bread, cut into cubes
3 tablespoons olive oil
3 garlic cloves, mashed
3 cups romaine lettuce, chopped
¼ cup grated Parmesan cheese
1 cup strawberries, diced
½ cup sliced black olives

Preheat oven to 350 degrees (F). Mash garlic into oil in a large bowl. Add bread cubes and toss to coat. Place on baking sheet and toast for 4 minutes. Prepare dressing below. Toss lettuce with bread croutons, strawberries, olives, and dressing. Top with Parmesan cheese.

Caesar Dressing

INGREDIENTS

¼ cup olive oil
3 tablespoons white vinegar
½ teaspoon salt

2 eggs
½ teaspoon black pepper
1 teaspoon Worcestershire sauce

Wisk ingredients and chill.

The produce section at the
grocery store is like a work of art...
all the tempting colors and shapes.
It's inspiring to find vegetables
that look so good you change
your dinner plans.

~Carolyn Coblentz

Chicken Salad with Sun-Dried Tomatoes, Spinach, and Feta Cheese

This is one of the many salads in this book that pair just a few ingredients for a major flavor punch. Serves well with pita bread or crustini, or as-is, warm or chilled.

Makes 4 servings

INGREDIENTS

2 chicken breasts, sliced into thin strips
½ teaspoon salt
¼ teaspoon pepper
3 cloves pressed garlic
1 small onion, chopped
2 tablespoons olive oil
½ cup sun-dried tomatoes in oil, drained and chopped
3 cups fresh spinach
12 ounces feta cheese, crumbled

Season chicken with salt and pepper. Cook with garlic and onions in oil over medium-high heat for approximately 6 minutes. Add the sun-dried tomatoes and spinach and cook, stirring frequently, for another 3 to 5 minutes, or until chicken is cooked through. Add feta and taste to adjust seasonings. Remove from heat and serve warm or chilled.

Sweet and Sour Chicken Salad with Apples

You may never make the same old, same old chicken salad again! The apples and onions provide the crunch, while the savory chicken and dressing balance things out to add up to a feast of flavors great for any season. This salad is delicious on rolls with lettuce, with crackers, or on a bed of greens.

Makes 4 servings

INGREDIENTS

3 chicken breasts, cubed
½ teaspoon salt
¼ teaspoon pepper
1 teaspoon poultry seasoning
1 tablespoon olive oil
2 apples, diced

½ onion, diced
4 tablespoons mango chutney*
3 tablespoons sour cream
2 teaspoons Dijon mustard
½ teaspoon garlic salt
½ teaspoon lemon juice

Season chicken with salt, pepper, and poultry seasoning. Heat oil in pan on stove. Cook chicken until cooked through; cool chicken completely. Mix with remaining ingredients.

Mango chutney is a sweet/spicy jelly-type relish sold in the condiments aisle at most grocery stores. If you can't find this, or you prefer, substitute a combination of apricot jam and spicy mustard. Recipes for homemade chutney are available on the Organizing Dinner website at www. organizingdinner.com

As the chopping begins,
a spirit of anticipation builds...
releasing smells, luring you to a quick taste,
and then...as your mound of vegetables
materializes, imagination unlocks the door
to the endless potential of salad.
You already feel accomplished knowing
that you will give a treat to both your
taste buds and your health.

~Carolyn Coblentz

13

Chopped Salad

Here's a salad that simply says "fun." It's easy to eat and great for large groups. It can also be eaten as a "salad sandwich" on ciabatta bread or other rolls.

Makes two large entrée salads, or a side serving for 4-6.

INGREDIENTS

1 cup small pasta noodles, such as orzo or ditalini
1 heart Romaine lettuce, finely chopped
1 avocado, diced
1 tomato, seeded, cored, and diced into small pieces
½ cup crumbled gorgonzola cheese
3 slices crisply cooked bacon, crumbled

Cook pasta according to package directions, rinse in cool water and drain. Mix all ingredients together and chill. Serve on large rolls or homemade bread. Serve with Parmesan Pepper dressing (below).

Parmesan Pepper Dressing

INGREDIENTS

½ cup sour cream
¾ cup lowfat buttermilk
½ cup grated Parmesan cheese
2 cloves garlic
6 tablespoons white wine vinegar
1 ½ tablespoons freshly ground black pepper
½ teaspoon salt

Wisk together ingredients and chill.

14

Couscous Salad

This yummy salad features the Mediterranean dish couscous, which is not a grain like some believe but is actually a coarsely ground semolina pasta that looks more like rice. Couscous is a good source of thiamine and niacin, and full of antioxidants. It's also fat-free and a good source of protein.

Makes 4 servings

INGREDIENTS

2 cups dry whole wheat couscous
2 tablespoons vegetable or chicken broth powder
¼ cup diced dried apricot
¼ cup raisins
¼ cup sliced almonds
3 tablespoons olive oil
3 tablespoons white vinegar
1 medium shallot, grated
2 tablespoons honey
¼ teaspoon rosemary
¼ teaspoon salt
2 tablespoons minced parsley

Cook couscous according to directions, adding the broth powder to the water. Cool and toss with apricots, raisins, and almonds. Combine olive oil, vinegar, shallot, honey, rosemary, and salt, and toss into couscous. Top with parsley and chill.

15

Bleu Cheese Potato Salad

Bypassing the most common way of serving potato salad — with mayonnaise —this salad combines vinegar with sour cream and bleu cheese for a deliciously creamy but light flavor delight.

Makes 8 servings

INGREDIENTS

3 pounds red potatoes
1 lemon
1 tablespoon salt
1 tablespoon vegetable or chicken broth powder (optional)
2 tablespoons Dijon mustard
¼ cup sour cream
2 tablespoons white wine vinegar
1 tablespoon minced dill
3 stalks celery, diced
¼ cup green onions, diced
½ cup crumbled bleu cheese

Dice potatoes, peel if desired, and place in large pot covered with cold water and salt. Bring to boil, add broth powder to pot, and cook 10 minutes or until potatoes are fork-tender. Rinse potatoes in cold water and then cover with juice of lemon. Stir together sour cream, mustard, vinegar, and dill and toss with potatoes. Add remaining ingredients and stir to blend. Season with additional salt and pepper if desired.

Perfect Pasta Salad

The perfection in this salad comes from the pasta process. Adding an acid, like lemon juice, right after rinsing seals the moisture right in to the pasta — both a fat-free way to free the pasta from sticking and a way to dramatically reduce the need for oil to add moisture.

Makes 4 servings

INGREDIENTS

8 ounces orzo or other small pasta
1 tablespoon lemon juice
1/8 cup balsamic vinegar
3 tablespoons olive oil
1 teaspoon oregano
1/2 teaspoon garlic salt
1 bell pepper, diced
1/2 cup kalamata olives, pitted and diced, including some of their liquid
1/4 cup onion, diced
4 ounces crumbled feta cheese

Cook pasta according to package directions. Strain and rinse with cold water. Top immediately with lemon juice to seal in moisture. Combine vinegar, oil, oregano, and garlic salt to make dressing. Add dressing and stir well. Toss in vegetables and cheese.

17

Sweet Potato Salad

Sweet potatoes are ranked as one of the healthiest vegetables on Earth. And their naturally beautiful color and sweet but rich taste make them family-friendly and a delight to eat. With higher fiber, protein, and more vitamins than a traditional spud, you'll be doing your family and friends a favor by offering this substitute to traditional potato salad.

Makes 8 servings

INGREDIENTS

6 cups sweet potatoes
(approximately 3–4) peeled,
and diced in ¾" cubes
2½ tablespoons vegetable oil

½ teaspoon salt
½ teaspoon pepper
¼ red onion, finely chopped

Put diced sweet potatoes into large mixing bowl and stir in oil, salt, and pepper to coat. Place coated potatoes on baking sheet in 375-degree (F) oven for 1 hour, turning at least once (edges should be brown and crispy). Remove from oven and cool completely. Combine potatoes with onions; toss with Maple Vinegar Dressing (below).

Maple Vinegar Dressing

INGREDIENTS

4 tablespoons Grade A
pure maple syrup
1 tablespoon olive oil
3 tablespoons balsamic vinegar

¼ cup fresh parsley leaves
1½ teaspoon spicy yellow mustard

Mix or blend ingredients.

Tuna Pea Pasta Salad

A simply great example of how simple can be great. The lime juice adds the lightness and flavor to this yummy dish.

Makes 4 servings

INGREDIENTS

8 ounces bowtie pasta noodles
6 ounces crumbled cooked tuna (fresh or canned in water, drained)
Juice of 1 lime
1 cup spring peas
½ onion, diced
¼ cup white vinegar
1 teaspoon Dijon mustard
1 tablespoon minced tarragon
1 teaspoon garlic salt
½ teaspoon black pepper
⅛ cup olive oil

Cook pasta according to package directions. Rinse in cold water and drain. Toss immediately with juice of one lime to seal in moisture. Add remaining ingredients, stir to combine well, and chill.

Wild Rice Cranberry Salad

This delicious salad is a great accompaniment to many a main course, combining your starches and vegetables in one dish. It is also a colorful addition to any buffet table.

Makes 4–6 servings

INGREDIENTS

2 cups long grain rice
1 cup wild rice
4 cups chicken or vegetable broth
3 green onions, sliced
2 cups spring peas
½ cup sesame seeds
¾ cup dried cranberries
2 tablespoons olive oil
2 tablespoons red wine vinegar
1 teaspoon sugar
½ teaspoon paprika

Add long grain and wild rice to the chicken broth in a medium saucepan. Bring to a boil, reduce heat to low, and cover. Let cook for 40 minutes. Remove from heat and cool completely. Whisk together the olive oil, red wine vinegar, sugar, and paprika to make dressing. In a large bowl, gently mix together the cooled cooked rice, green onions, peas, dried cranberries, sesame seeds, and dressing.

Elizabeth Berry once said
"Shipping is a terrible thing to do to vegetables,
they probably get jet-lagged just like people."
It may take some work, but if you put your
mind to it, finding fresh, local ingredients
may be easier than you think.
Storing vegetables and herbs in plastic bags
in a cool place helps maintain
their freshness, and health value.

- Kelly Donlea

Sun-Dried Tomato Egg Salad

This dish proves that egg salad doesn't need to be ordinary! This recipe teams tangy sun-dried tomatoes with crisp minced chives to bring life, color, and excitement to an always easy creation.

Makes 4 servings

INGREDIENTS

1 dozen eggs
1 teaspoon salt
3 tablespoons mustard
3 tablespoons Greek yogurt
3 tablespoons sour cream
¼ cup vinegar
¼ cup celery, diced
¼ cup sun-dried tomato pieces, sliced
⅛ cup chives, minced

In large pot, cover eggs in water and add 1 teaspoon salt. Bring to a rapid boil and reduce heat to low; simmer for 15 minutes. Rinse eggs in cold water, drain, and cool completely. Peel and dice eggs. Separately, combine mustard, yogurt, sour cream and vinegar. Add mustard mixture and remaining ingredients to eggs and stir. Chill before serving.

Made for
a Meal

21

Shrimp, Avocado, and Mango Salad

If you could taste a beach (no, not the sand, but the beauty, freshness and fun), this salad would be it. Here, we pair light ingredients together for a salad that's filling and high in protein.

Makes two large entrée salads, or a side serving for 4–6.

INGREDIENTS

1 pound shrimp, peeled and de-veined
(raw or precooked; your preference)
1 tablespoon salt
3 tablespoons red onion, diced
3 limes for precooked shrimp (6 for raw)

1 cucumber, seeded and diced
1 avocado, diced
½ mango, diced
1 heart romaine lettuce, chopped
1 tablespoon cilantro, minced

Dice shrimp and place in dish. Season with salt, top with onion, and squeeze with juice from limes (3 if cooked, 6 if raw). For cooked shrimp, let marinate at least one-half hour, up to 8 hours. If shrimp is uncooked, let shrimp "cook" in lime juice for at least 3 hours, up to overnight. Add avocado and mango to shrimp, and serve on bed of lettuce topped with cilantro and Green Goddess dressing (below).

Green Goddess Dressing

INGREDIENTS

½ cup Greek yogurt
2 tablespoons white wine vinegar
Juice of 1 lime
1 teaspoon garlic salt
2 tablespoons fresh basil, chopped
2 tablespoons fresh dill, chopped

Combine ingredients and chill.

22

Spinach and Asiago Asparagus Salad

Elegant and unique, this salad combines warm melted cheese with crisp, fresh spinach for a creamy yet crunchy salad that will linger on the taste buds long after it's gone.

Makes two large entrée salads, or a side serving for 4–6.

INGREDIENTS

1 teaspoon olive oil
1 teaspoon balsamic vinegar
½ pound asparagus
(approximately 8 spears)

⅓ cup Asiago cheese
6 slices prosciutto
3 cups spinach leaves

Coat a pan on stove with one teaspoon olive oil and one teaspoon balsamic vinegar. Add garlic and asparagus to pan. Stir to coat and cook 4 minutes, until slightly tender. Sprinkle asparagus with Asiago cheese. Continue cooking until cheese is melted. Cool completely and cut into 1-inch pieces. Place asparagus and prosciutto on top of spinach leaves and toss with remaining cheese and Green Goddess dressing (below).

Green Goddess Dressing

INGREDIENTS

½ cup Greek yogurt
2 tablespoons white wine vinegar
Juice of 1 lime
1 teaspoon garlic salt
2 tablespoons fresh basil, chopped
2 tablespoons fresh dill, chopped

Combine ingredients and chill.

"Cooking Southwest is a lot like
cooking out of 70 Meals, One Trip to the Store. . .
each recipe pulls from the same pool of ingredients.
That made it all the more rewarding
to come up with this delicious salad, by
pairing traditional Southwest ingredients
in a unique way."

~ Kelly Donlea

23

Southwest Cornbread Salad

One of Organizing Dinner's most popular appetizers, Mamaschetta, combines cornbread, black beans, tomatoes, avocados, and flavorful herbs. When translated into a salad, the combo makes for a great take on taco salad that is...anything but ordinary.

Makes two large entrée salads, or a side serving for 4–6.

INGREDIENTS

2 cups lettuce
1 tomato, diced
1 can black beans, drained and rinsed
2 tablespoons red onion, diced
2 tablespoons olive oil
1 tablespoon balsamic vinegar

1 teaspoon garlic salt
½ teaspoon oregano
½ teaspoon finely diced parsley
2 cups cornbread, cubed
1 avocado, diced

Combine tomato, black beans, and onion with oil, vinegar, and seasonings/spices. In large bowl, top lettuce with black bean mixture, cornbread, avocado and Fiesta Dressing (below).

Fiesta Dressing

INGREDIENTS

1 cup sour cream
⅓ cup milk
½ cup salsa
⅛ cup fresh chopped cilantro

Combine all ingredients and chill.

24

Broccoli and Cauliflower Tortellini Salad

This rich and filling pasta salad is hearty enough to stand on its own as a meal or as a side dish at your next barbeque.

Makes two large entrée salads or a side serving for 4–6.

INGREDIENTS

5 slices bacon
¾ cup balsamic vinegar
2 tablespoons sugar
1 tablespoon Dijon mustard
8 ounces cheese tortellini
juice of one lemon
2 cups broccoli florets
2 cups cauliflower florets
1½ cups cherry tomatoes, seeded and diced

Cook tortellini according to package directions. Drain, rinse, and cover with juice of one lemon. Reserve. Fry bacon in deep pan until crisp. Remove bacon from pan and drain on paper towels. Drain all but 1 tablespoon oil from pan. Bring heat to low and whisk vinegar, sugar, and mustard into pan. Remove from heat and cool for dressing. Meanwhile, in boiling water, blanch cauliflower and broccoli for 2 minutes. Rinse immediately with cold water and drain. Toss tortellini and broccoli/cauliflower with bacon, tomatoes, and dressing. Chill or serve immediately at room temperature.

"Did you ever stop to taste a carrot?
Not just eat it, but taste it?
You can't taste the beauty and
energy of the earth in a Twinkie."

~ Astrid Alauda

25

Crab Cobb Salad

What do you get when you cross a stuffed tomato with a Cobb salad? You get this delightful creation that is just bursting with good health and great flavor.

Makes two large entrée salad or a side serving for 4–6.

INGREDIENTS

2 cups lettuce
2 tomatoes, sliced
1 cup lump crabmeat
1 avocado, sliced
2 hard-boiled eggs, sliced
2 pieces bacon, crumbled
½ cup cheddar or crumbled bleu cheese
Honey Mustard Dressing

In large bowl, top lettuce with crabmeat, avocado, egg, bacon and cheese. Serve with Honey Mustard Dressing (below). Substitute Bleu Cheese Dressing if you prefer (recipe on page 77).

Honey Mustard Dressing

INGREDIENTS

5 tablespoons honey
3 tablespoons Dijon mustard
2 tablespoons white vinegar
1 tablespoon oil
½ teaspoon black pepper

Combine ingredients and chill.

26

Grilled Teriyaki Salmon and Citrus Salad

This hearty salad makes a wonderful, filling meal. We pair teriyaki salmon with fresh mandarin oranges, grapefruit, and almonds to give this salad some zing!

Makes 4 entrée salads

INGREDIENTS

1 grapefruit, peeled
¾ cup mandarin oranges, halved
3 cups mixed greens

3 tablespoons diced Green onion
3 tablespoons shaved almonds
2 salmon fillets

Teriyaki Marinade

INGREDIENTS

3 tablespoons soy sauce
2 tablespoons cooking sherry
or rice vinegar
2 tablespoons honey

2 cloves garlic, minced
1 teaspoon ginger, minced
1 teaspoon mustard

Combine ingredients for marinade in a zip-close bag. Add salmon and marinate in refrigerator for at least one half hour. Discard marinade and grill salmon over high heat, approximately 4 minutes per side, until cooked through. Halve salmon fillets and cool. Top greens with green onions, almonds, fruit, and salmon. Serve with Lemon Garlic Dressing.

Lemon Garlic Dressing

INGREDIENTS

3 tablespoons sour cream
1 teaspoon mustard
½ teaspoon garlic salt

½ teaspoon pepper
1 teaspoon lemon juice
1 teaspoon white vinegar

27

Pizza Salad

It's high time these two staples of the American menu crossed paths. With filling pizza dough breadsticks and zesty diced tomatoes, you once again have a salad hearty enough for a meal.

Makes 3 large entrée salads or a side serving for 6–8.

INGREDIENTS

3 cups flour
1 package or ¼ ounce yeast
3 tablespoons olive oil
1 cup hot water
Salt
1 teaspoon garlic salt
1 ½ teaspoons dried oregano
4 cups lettuce, chopped
1 can diced tomatoes, lightly drained

½ package button mushrooms, sliced
3 ounces fresh mozzarella cheese, cut into half-size chunks
3 ounces pepperoni chunks or slices
¼ cup balsamic vinegar
¼ cup olive oil
3 tablespoons Parmesan cheese

Combine yeast, 1 teaspoon salt, and 2 cups flour in a large bowl. Separately, combine water and 3 tablespoons olive oil. Add the water/oil mixture to the flour mixture and combine thoroughly with hands or mixer. Knead in remaining 1 cup flour to form dough. Cover and let rise 15 minutes. Punch down dough and knead on floured surface. Break off small fistfuls and roll into breadstick shapes. Line breadsticks on greased cookie sheet and sprinkle with garlic, salt, and oregano. Bake at 375 degrees (F) for 12 minutes. Let breadsticks cool completely. Meanwhile, arrange tomatoes, pepperoni, cheese, and mushrooms on bed of lettuce. Break breadsticks into 1-inch pieces and arrange around the outer edges of salad. Combine olive oil, balsamic vinegar, and Parmesan cheese with 1 teaspoon dried oregano and serve as dressing.

28

Spicy Peanut Noodle Salad

In this salad, we pair the smooth flavors of a great peanut satay with the crunch of fresh vegetables and the sturdiness of linguini. The result makes for a salad you won't get enough of! Serve topped with grilled chicken or shrimp or as a stand-alone meal.

Makes 6 servings

INGREDIENTS

6 tablespoons peanut butter
¼ cup vegetable or chicken broth
3 tablespoons white vinegar
3 tablespoons soy sauce
1½ tablespoons sugar
1 tablespoon sesame oil
1 tablespoon minced ginger
½ teaspoon cayenne pepper
8 ounces linguini
1 large orange bell pepper, cut into matchstick-size strips
½ cup chopped green onions
5 large lettuce leaves
¼ cup chopped fresh cilantro
¼ cup chopped salted peanuts

Combine first 8 ingredients in small bowl; whisk to blend. Set dressing aside. Cook pasta in large pot of boiling salted water until just tender but still firm to bite, stirring occasionally. Drain pasta; rinse with cold water and drain again. Transfer pasta to medium bowl. Add bell pepper and green onions. Toss salad with dressing; season with salt and pepper. Line serving bowl with lettuce leaves and transfer salad to prepared bowl. Sprinkle with cilantro and peanuts.

29

Pasadena Pomegranate Salad

This delicious salad has a fresh crispness to it that is simply bursting with the feel of California living. Because Cali is one of the few places with weather temperate enough to cultivate pomegranates, we credit the state in naming this tasty salad. Fortunately California's produce can be found in most areas, so those of us who don't live there can pretend.

Makes two large entrée salads, or a side serving for 4–6.

INGREDIENTS

Seeds of one-half pomegranate
2 cups hearty lettuce (such as arugula)
2 chicken breasts
1 teaspoon seasoning salt
1 teaspoon garlic powder

1 teaspoon pepper
Juice of one lime
2 tablespoons olive oil
½ cup chopped pecans
1 avocado, sliced

Season chicken breasts with seasoning salt, garlic powder, and pepper. In a covered dish, or a Zip-close bag, place chicken, juice of one lime and oil. Marinate for at least one half hour in refrigerator. Grill chicken or sear in pan on stove until cooked through. Cool and slice. In a large bowl, place chicken on top of lettuce. Top with pomegranate seeds, cheese, pecans, and avocado slices. Serve with pomegranate dressing (below).

Pomegranate Dressing

Seeds of one-half pomegranate
2 tablespoons cider vinegar
2 tablespoons honey

½ teaspoon garlic salt
2 teaspoons Dijon mustard
½ teaspoon black pepper

Mash half pomegranate in a bowl and pass through strainer, reserving just the juice. Combine pomegranate juice with vinegar, honey, garlic salt, mustard, and pepper, and whisk.

30

Tuna Mango Salad

The rich saltiness of tuna combined with the light zest of mango makes for a delightful flavor combination. Like traditional tuna salad, this works great as a sandwich or with crackers, or it can also be served beautifully in a tortilla.

Makes 4 servings

INGREDIENTS

12 ounces crumbled cooked tuna (fresh tuna steaks are best; canned tuna in water (drained) also works)
One-half mango, peeled and cubed
One-half cucumber, peeled, seeded, and cubed
¼ cup diced onion
1 teaspoon dry mustard
4 tablespoons sesame oil
1 tablespoon soy sauce
1 tablespoon honey
2 tablespoons lime juice
2 teaspoons chopped fresh cilantro
1 teaspoon salt
½ teaspoon pepper

If using fresh tuna steaks, cook until medium well; cool and crumble. Combine tuna with mango, cucumber, and onion. Whisk together remaining ingredients and blend with tuna. Chill.

"Dressing our own salads is a bit
of a lost art. It is so easy to keep basic
salad dressing ingredients on hand.
In fact, most of us probably have oil,
vinegar, mustard or yogurt,
and some seasonings and herbs
at home all the time.
Coming back to dressing our own salads
saves us from unneeded processed
ingredients and preservatives.
And learning how to "season" a salad
with flavorful ingredients and seasonings
saves us from the need to
add excess oils or other fats.
That's what 30 Spectacular Salads
is all about."

~ Kelly Donlea

Dressings and Accompaniments

1

Asian Dressing

INGREDIENTS

¼ cup sugar
½ cup white vinegar
¾ cup oil
3 tablespoons soy sauce

Bring first three ingredients to a boil in pot on stove, stirring frequently. Remove from heat, whisk in soy sauce, and chill.

2

Basil Dressing

INGREDIENTS

1 tablespoon olive oil
2 tablespoons vinegar
3 fresh basil leaves, finely chopped
⅛ teaspoon pepper
¼ teaspoon salt
2 teaspoons lemon juice
1 large clove garlic, pressed

Combine all ingredients in food processor and chill.

3

Bleu Cheese Dressing

INGREDIENTS

⅛ cup sour cream
½ cup Greek yogurt
4 ounces bleu cheese crumbles
1 tablespoon Worcestershire sauce
3 tablespoons white vinegar

Combine ingredients and chill.

Buttermilk Ranch Dressing

INGREDIENTS

1 cup buttermilk
½ cup sour cream
1 teaspoon lemon or lime juice
⅛ teaspoon paprika
¼ teaspoon mustard powder
½ teaspoon salt

⅛ teaspoon black pepper
1 tablespoon chopped fresh parsley
1 teaspoon chopped fresh chives
¼ teaspoon dry dill (or 1 teaspoon chopped fresh)

Combine all ingredients and chill.

Caesar Dressing

INGREDIENTS

¼ cup olive oil
3 tablespoons white vinegar
½ teaspoon salt
2 eggs, pasteurized (optional)
½ teaspoon black pepper
1 teaspoon Worcestershire sauce
¼ cup Parmesan cheese

Wisk together all ingredients and chill.

Fiesta Dressing

INGREDIENTS

1 cup yogurt
⅓ cup milk
½ cup salsa
⅛ cup fresh chopped cilantro

Combine sour cream, milk, seasonings, and salsa. Top with cilantro.

7

Garlic Croutons

INGREDIENTS

4 tablespoons butter or oil
1 clove garlic, minced
3 (¾-inch thick) slices French bread, cut into cubes

Preheat oven to 350 degrees (F). In a large sauté pan, melt butter over medium heat. Mash garlic into melted butter or oil. Add bread cubes and toss to coat. Place on baking sheet and toast for 4 minutes. Cool and serve with your favorite salad.

8

Green Goddess Dressing

INGREDIENTS

½ cup Greek yogurt
2 tablespoons white wine vinegar
Juice of 1 lime
1 teaspoon garlic salt
2 tablespoons fresh basil, chopped
2 tablespoons fresh dill, chopped

Combine all ingredients and chill.

9

Honey Mustard Dressing

INGREDIENTS

5 tablespoons honey
3 tablespoons Dijon mustard
2 tablespoons white vinegar
1 tablespoon oil
½ teaspoon black pepper

Whisk all ingredients together and chill.

10

Italian Dressing

INGREDIENTS

½ teaspoon garlic salt
½ teaspoon onion powder
½ teaspoon white sugar
1 tablespoon dried oregano
½ teaspoon ground black pepper
½ teaspoon dried basil

1 teaspoon dried parsley
1 tablespoon salt
3 tablespoons white vinegar
⅓ cup oil
1 tablespoon water

Whisk all ingredients together and chill.

11

Lemon Garlic Dressing

INGREDIENTS

3 tablespoons sour cream
1 teaspoon mustard
½ teaspoon garlic salt
½ teaspoon pepper
1 teaspoon lemon juice
1 teaspoon white vinegar

Whisk all ingredients together and chill.

12

Maple Vinegar Dressing

INGREDIENTS

4 tablespoons Grade A pure maple syrup
1 tablespoon olive oil
3 tablespoons white balsamic vinegar
¼ cup fresh parsley leaves
1½ teaspoon spicy yellow mustard

Whisk all ingredients together and chill.

Parmesan Pepper Dressing

INGREDIENTS

½ cup sour cream
¾ cup lowfat buttermilk
½ cup grated Parmesan cheese
2 cloves garlic
6 tablespoons white wine vinegar
1 tablespoon freshly ground black pepper
½ teaspoon salt

Combine all ingredients in a food processor until smooth.

Pomegranate Dressing

INGREDIENTS

Seeds of one-half pomegranate
2 tablespoons cider vinegar
2 tablespoons honey
½ teaspoon garlic salt
2 teaspoons Dijon mustard
½ teaspoon black pepper

Mash the seeds of half a pomegranate in a bowl and pass through strainer, reserving just the juice. Combine pomegranate juice with vinegar, honey, garlic salt, mustard, and pepper. Whisk.

Teriyaki Marinade

INGREDIENTS

3 tablespoons soy sauce
2 tablespoons cooking sherry
or rice vinegar
2 tablespoons honey

Combine all ingredients and use for marinade.

From our delighted customers...

"This cookbook redefines salad as an adventure and empowers people to go beyond the preconceived notion of what salad is. The recipes are dynamic and the food delicious. Each salad provides a delicate balance of flavor, texture, and flair. They are perfect for entertaining but simple enough to make on a Tuesday night. My family loves these salads!"

— *Jean Masukevich*
  Bending Toward the Light

....

"I have had the pleasure of feasting on Kelly's salads with my camera lens and with my family at mealtime. These salads are beautiful to look at and satisfying to serve. The elements of Kelly's salads are diverse and luscious — crispy greens, fresh fruit, savory cheeses, and zesty dressings all pack a flavorful punch at the dinner hour while keeping you on a nutritious pathway. Kelly is passionate about getting cooks of all degrees into their kitchens and making them successful. This cookbook is a valuable tool for every home chef looking for both tried-and-true and unique and flavorful salad options. My copy of *30 Spectacular Salads* will be referenced for many years to come"

— *Kristin Enstrom*
  Enstrom & Wheat
  30 Spectacular Salads Food Photographer